Day of the Dead
A Pictorial Archive of Día de Los Muertos

Selected and Edited by Jean Moss

DOVER PUBLICATIONS, INC.
MINEOLA, NEW YORK

Bibliographical Note
Day of the Dead: A Pictorial Archive of Día de Los Muertos is a new work, first published by Dover Publications, Inc. in 2010.

DOVER *Pictorial Archive* SERIES

International Standard Book Number
ISBN-13: 978-0-486-48026-8
ISBN-10: 0-486-48026-7

    The accompanying CD-ROM contains 600 dpi TIFF files, and both high- and low-resolution JPEG files of each individual image. Although some of the images have been cropped for graphic effect in the book, the entire image is offered on the CD-ROM. The ☐Images☐folder on the CD contains two different folders. All of the high-resolution files have been placed in one folder, and the Internet-ready files are in another folder. Every image has a unique file name in the following format: xxx.JPG. The first 3 digits of the file name, before the period, correspond to the number printed under the image in the book. The last 3 letters of the file name ☐JPG,☐refer to the file format. So, 001.JPG would be the first file in the folder.
    Also included on the CD-ROM is Dover Design Manager, a simple graphics editing program for Windows that will allow you to view, print, crop, and rotate the images.

For technical support, contact:
  Telephone: 1 (617) 249-0245
  Fax: 1 (617) 249-0245
  Email: dover@artimaging.com
  Internet: http://www.dovertechsupport.com
  The fastest way to receive technical support is via email or the Internet.

DESIGN BY ALAN WELLER
Manufactured in the United States by Courier Corporation
48026704   2015
www.doverpublications.com

Preface

It is late October. Trucks, full and overflowing with bright orange, many-petaled marigolds, deep red, velvety cockscombs, and delicate, lacy white baby's breath, travel the back roads and deliver their cargo to the markets in villages, towns, and cities. The markets are busier than usual, bustling with crowded stalls selling pottery, flowers, colorful paper cutouts, toys in shapes of skeletons and skulls, and sugar in many fanciful shapes. Today there are special markets, where last week there was only an open field, a large plaza, or an empty public courtyard. Women and children hurry home with large bundles of flowers on their heads. All of Mexico is preparing for Los Dias de los Muertos, the Days of the Dead, when the living invite the dead to return, to serve as messengers between the living and the gods, to share a feast with them, and to reunite in family and community.

The history of the celebration, the thousands of customs and practices throughout the country, the psychology of the Mexican people and their attitude toward death, and the art that has developed from the holiday, are so deep, so multi-layered, and so complex that I can touch only the surface in this preface.

Although customs vary from urban areas to rural, from region to region, and even from to village to village, the celebration of the Days of the Dead is practiced throughout Mexico. Most normal activities are suspended. Homes are cleaned and altars are created in the main room. Sometimes there are special altars dedicated to those in the family who have died in the past year. Some altars are dedicated to all in the family who have passed, with separate altars for adults and children. The altars are decorated with paper cutouts and flowers. Often marigold petals are scattered from the altar to the door and out into the street, sometimes even to a nearby cemetery, creating a path for the spirits to find their way home. There are candles to light the way for the returning souls. When possible, photographs of the deceased are placed on the altar. Fruit, tamales, special breads, varieties of mole, chocolate, and water are always offered for the returning dead, and beloved objects are placed on the altar to help them feel at home—cigarettes, Coca Cola, mescal or tequila, a sombrero, an apron, or toys for the departed children. And always, the Virgin, usually Our Lady of Guadalupe and other saints watch over the altar while incense burns on the ground in front of it.

Most Mexican cemeteries do not have grounds keepers, and all preparation for the Days of the Dead is taken on by the community and individual families. The cemeteries are cleaned, and many are decorated with flower arches and communal altars. If the cemeteries are adjacent to a church, the church is decorated also. Families weed the grave sites and scrub or paint the tombstones. They decorate the graves with flowers and candles—at least one for each returning soul. If there are graves with no surviving family, members of the community may also clean and place flowers and food on them.

November 1st is the day when the children, the *angelitos*, return, and November 2nd is the day for returning adults. Both of these days are celebrated in the home and at the cemetery. Food and drink are usually brought to the graves, as are other offerings. Candles are lit, and sometimes there are small bonfires for warmth and light. Strolling musicians play the favorite songs of the departed. All-night vigils are kept in the cemeteries. Women pray and gossip. Men keep watch, drink, and gossip. Children play with the new toys bought for them during this holiday time.

In Mexico City and other urban areas of Mexico, the celebration is not as devout and solemn. Much of the religious sense is absent and the celebration is festive, often raucous, even defiant towards death. It is more a day for remembrance of the dead than a day of actual communication with them. The attitude is generally more aesthetic, artistic and intellectual, than religious. There are altars in restaurants, museums, and community centers, often built by professional and recognized artists. Skulls and skeletons, which are seldom seen in rural or indigenous communities, abound.

Spanish Dictionaries define the word *calavera* simply as "skull." Exactly when and how in Mexico the word extended to mean an entire skeleton is not known, but by the late nineteenth century, the word was in general use as a reference to the depiction of skeletons by artists such as Manuel Manilla, Jose Guadalupe Posada, and others. Calaveras also refers to the poems written for the Day of Dead broadsheets which generally had a humorous or satirical point of view in criticism of current custom or politics. In the later part of the nineteenth century, it was customary for workers, such as shoe cleaners and road sweepers, to ask for their calavera (a donation of money) during the Days of the Dead. This custom later developed into one for children, who would then use the money to buy sweets. The onomatopoetic word *calaca* is another Mexican word for skeleton that is not to be found in Spanish dictionaries but is commonly used to describe the skeleton figures made throughout the country not only for the Days of the Dead, but during the year. The figures are made of carved wood, papier-maché, ceramic, sugar paste, or carved bone, and are generally depicted as joyous, wearing festive clothing and flowers, dancing or playing music. And, in the wonderful way that language evolves, in the last few years, I have heard people in different parts of the country, with different educational backgrounds, refer to all female skeleton figures as *catrinas*. This refers to the 1913 iconographic lithograph by Jose Guadalupe Posada of a calavera of a fashionable lady wearing a large flowered and plumed hat. She was later known as "La Calavera Catrina" (from *catrin* which means elegant) by the post-revolutionary artists of the mid-twentieth century, and Diego Rivera recreated her as a central figure in his mural, "Dream of a Sunday Afternoon in Alameda Park."

As early as the mid-eighteenth century, there are accounts of the sale of sugar paste figures of animals, coffins, and saints during the Days of the Dead. The custom of placing toys on the graves of deceased children for them to play with on their brief yearly return is probably an ancient one. And we know that the current custom of making Day of the Dead toys for living children was in existence by the middle of the nineteenth century. Children love to play with these toys of miniature altars and burial scenes, tiered tombs, and calaveras engaged in daily life—as vendors or policemen, priests and nuns, or lovers and bridal couples. There are coffins in which a skeleton rises when you open the lid, stick puppet skeletons that play instruments when you pull a string, and skulls with movable jaws. There are figures of skeletons performing in every imaginable task of life.

In most, if not all, of the Mexican pre-Columbian cultures, death was an integral part of their life and religion. Death, human sacrifice, war, and rebirth were all a part of the equilibrium of their universe. The iconography of death in the form of skulls and skeletons appears in codices, seals, sculptures, on pottery, and in wall paintings. In pre-Hispanic times, there were many ways and times throughout the year to honor the deceased, but a major celebration happened to coincide with the European All Saints Day, and it is generally recognized that these two holidays merged to become the present intense celebration that is known as the Days of the Dead.

With the Spanish colonization of Mexico, came the European iconography of Death. Death was usually portrayed as a skeleton carrying a scythe and an hourglass and often wearing a hooded cloak. There were, among other images, those of the Dance of Death, the Ages of Man, and the Tree of Life, which included the figure of Death as a part of life.

In 1792, Joaquín de Bolaños, a friar from Zacatecas, published a fantastical work called "The Portentous Life of Death...." The accompanying engravings by Francisco Agüera Bustamente, were not terrifying and solemn like the European imagery, but were humorous, even frivolous. The author says in his prologue, "Death is unbridled, but in order to sweeten her memory, I present her gilded or disguised with a touch of jest, novelty, or grace... for I wish to amuse you with a little bit of mysticism, for I also seek to undeceive you; separate the gold from the dross, profit from what is serious, laugh at what is ridiculous." Truly an attitude towards death that has survived the succeeding centuries in Mexico.

With the independence of Mexico from Spain in 1821, there was greater freedom of the press, and although there were constraints of different kinds due to political turmoil, caricature became a popular medium of expression and along with it the depiction of the calavera in social and political commentary. In the year 1847, a play by the Spanish playwright Jose Zorilla arrived in Mexico. The play, "Don Juan Tenorio," is a version of the classic story of Don Juan in which much of the action takes place in a cemetery where statues and spirits come to life. It became a popular play, often performed during the Days of the Dead, and the character of Don Juan entered into the canon of calavera caricature. By the end of the nineteenth century, artists were using calavera figures to illustrate the poems and broadsides produced during the Day of Dead season which commented on political and social events of the time. Among these artists were the great Manuel Manilla and Jose Guadalupe Posada.*

In the years following the Mexican Revolution (1910–1920), artists, intellectuals, and politicians turned away from European culture and began a quest for what they felt was truly Mexican. Pre-Hispanic and indigenous culture and folk art were reconsidered. Foreigners, such as Jean Charlot, Pablo O'Higgins, and Francis Toor, who saw the popular and ancient art of Mexico with new eyes, were influential on the Mexican-born artists and writers. Posada became the master and inspiration for many of the great Mexican artists of the mid-twentieth century. In 1937 a group of artists led by Leopoldo Méndez and Pablo O'Higgins founded the "Taller de Gráfica Popular" or the "Peoples Graphic Workshop," known as the "TGP." Its stated mission was "to benefit by its works the progressive and democratic interests of the Mexican people, especially in the fight against fascist reaction." Most of the contemporary great Mexican artists of the time were involved and, working mostly in woodcut and linocut, they produced posters, portfolios, individual prints, and special publications. The influence of the rediscovered Manilla and Posada was enormous and many special publications were issued in which the exclusive use of the calavera provided the satirical comment on Mexican and international political and social situations.

The creation of objects associated with the Day of the Dead rituals has, in the last twenty or thirty years, taken on new dimensions. Museum exhibitions of Mexican folk art have highlighted the importance of the Day of Dead in the folk art tradition. These exhibitions, a plethora of books, international dealers in folk art, and Mexican government agencies promoting tourism and the popular art of Mexico have all helped to generate interest in both the public and private collection of this art form. Artists who were once anonymous, have now achieved "Grand Master" status. The international fascination with Mexico's Days of the Dead has brought a little more prosperity to some communities and artisans.

Before the conquest and to the present, the concept of duality has been part of the foundation of Mexican culture—the eternal flow between opposites in the cycle of life in which death is an integral part. Since death is a part of life you cannot escape it. You must acknowledge it. You must reverence it or mock it—or both.

* For more detailed information on Manilla and Posada see:
Posada's Popular Mexican Prints (0-486-22854-1),
Dover Publications, Inc.

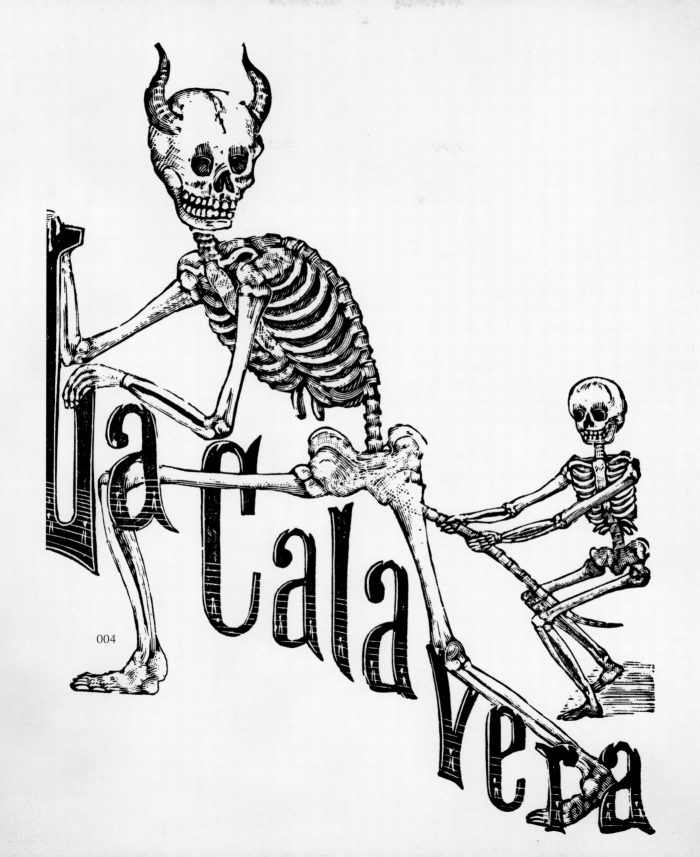

007

 CALAVERAS TELEVISIOSAS

todo por un hoyito

008

009

010

011

012

013

014

015

018

CIRCO, MAROMA Y TEATRO

019

22

021

022

24

023

024

025

026

027

028

029

031

032

033

034

037

038

039

040

041

042

043

044

047

048

049

050

051

052

053

054

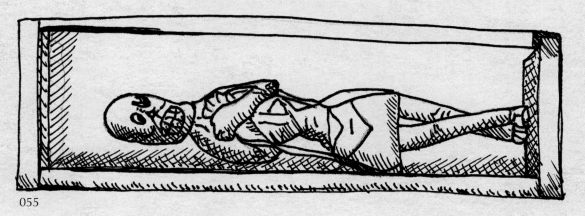

055

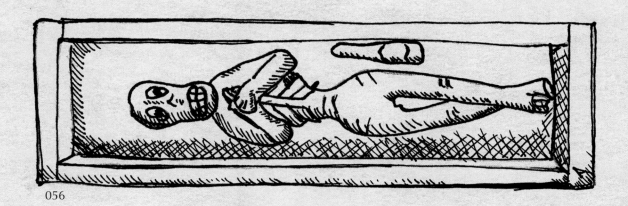

056

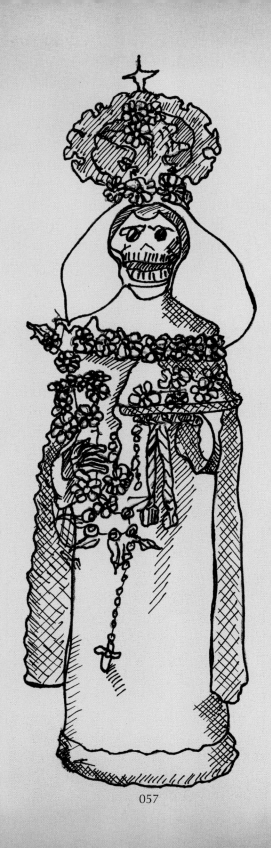

057

058

059

060

061

062

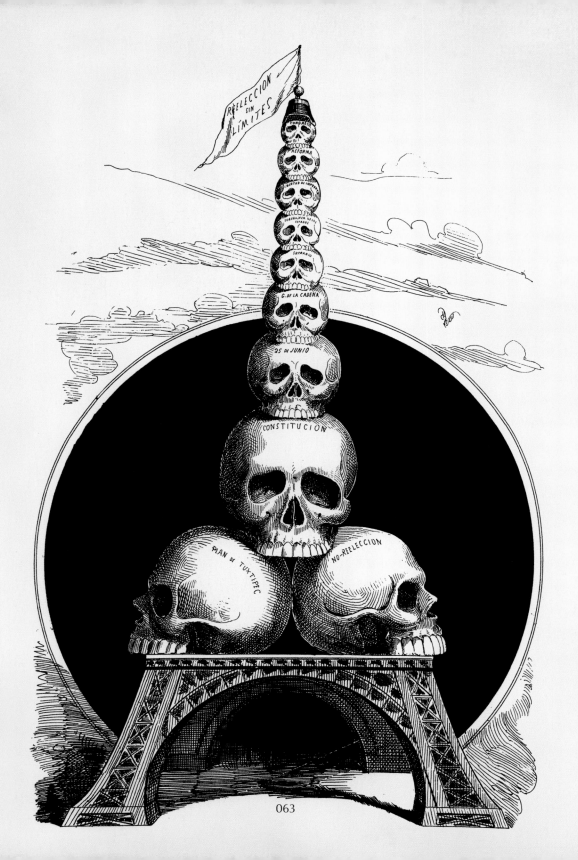

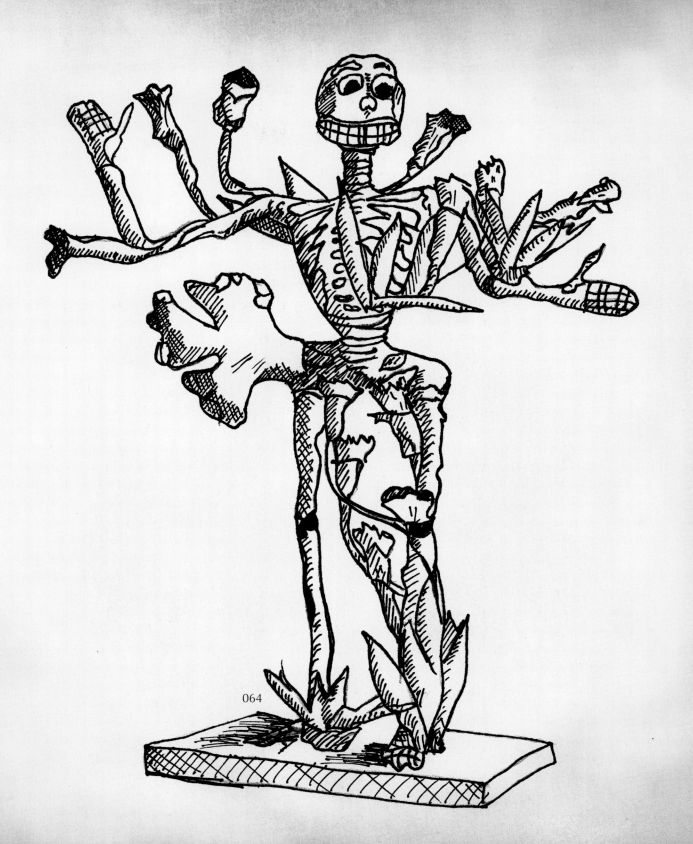

064

065

066

067

49

068

069

070

071

073

074

075

54

076

077

078

079

081

082

083

084

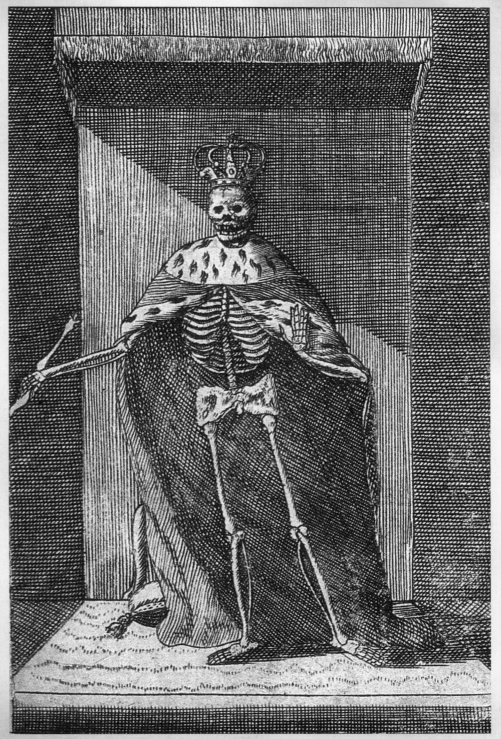

085

086

087

088

089

090

091

092

093

095

096

097

098

099

100

101

102

103

104

105

106

109

"YA NI EN LA PAZ DE LOS SEPULCROS CREO..."

110

111

112

114

115

116

117

119

120

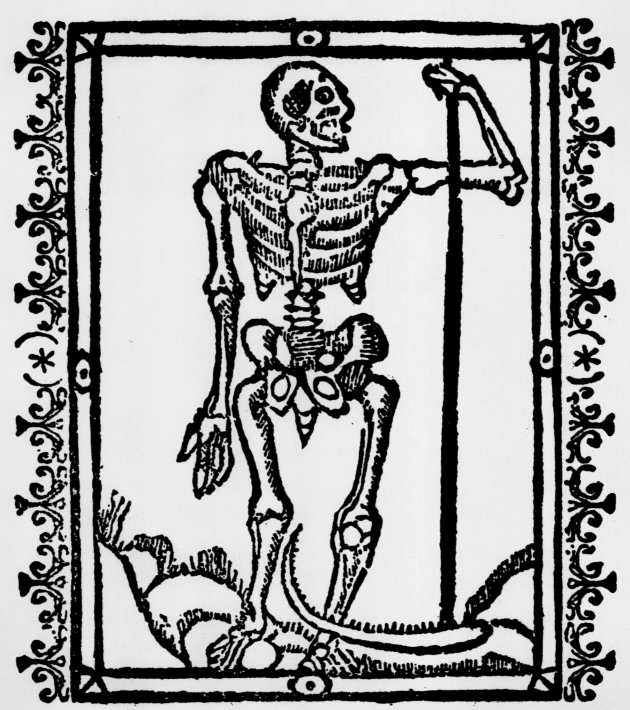

121

122

123

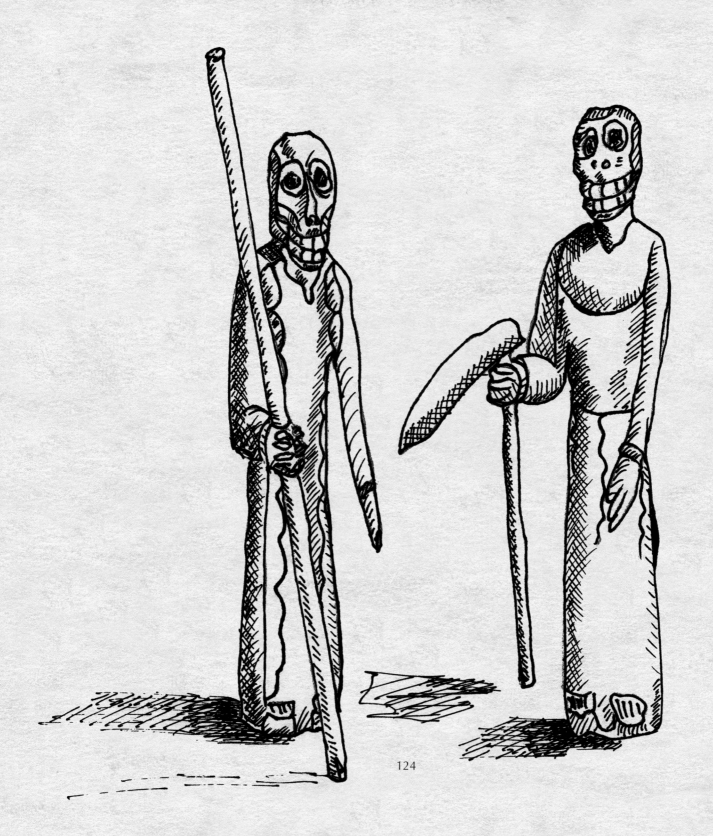

124

125

126

127

130

129

LA BOHEMIA DE LA MUERTE

131

132

133

134

135

138

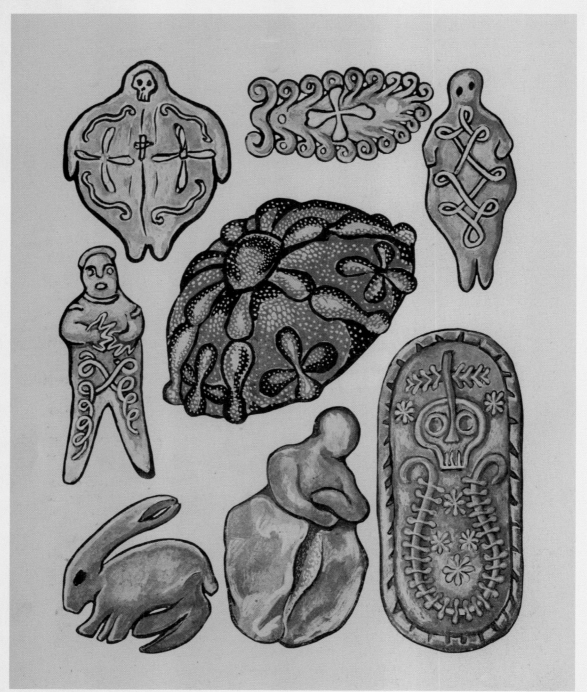

139

140

143

144

145

146

147

CALAVERAS RESURRECTAS

AQUI LES TRAIGO SU ROLLO DE SECAS Y MONTONERAS ENDIABLADAS CALAVERAS QUE SE SALIERON DEL HOYO

16 AÑOS DE CALAVERAS POLITICAS del TALLER de GRAFICA POPULAR

148

103

149

150

151

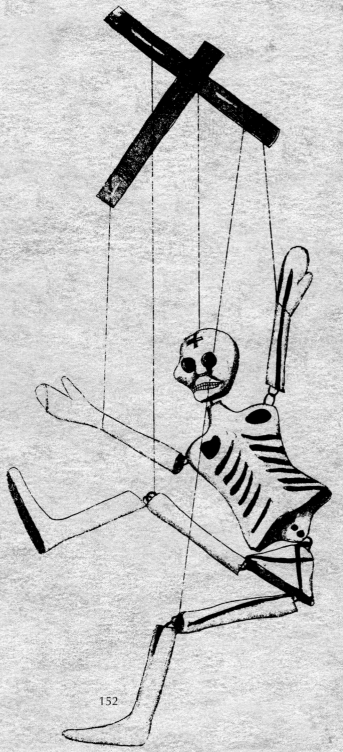

152

153

154

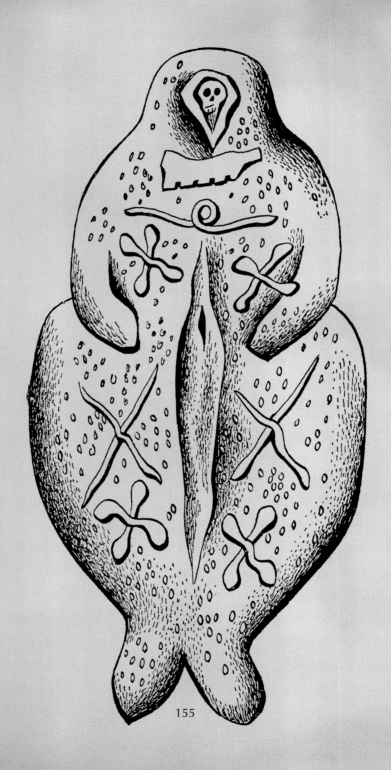

155

156

157

158

159

160

163

164

165

166

167

168

169

170

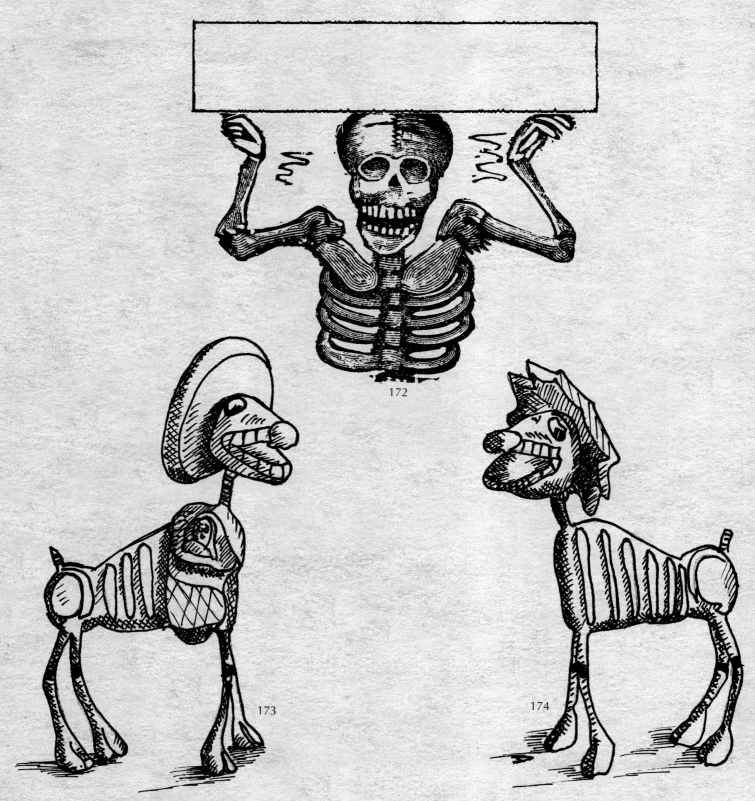

172

173

174

175

176

177

178

179

183

184

185

List of Images

001. Alan Crane. *Night of the Dead. Janitzio.* Lithograph. 1958.
002. Julio de la Fuente. Periodical Illustration. 1936.
003. J. G. Posada. *Calavera of Don Follas and the Negro.* (These were characters from traditional children's plays.) Broadsheet. Early 20th c.
004. M. Manilla. *The Infernal Calavera.* Broadsheet. Late 19th c.
005. Leopoldo Méndez. *Hoof and Mouth Disease Calaveras with Nylon Stockings.* Illustration for a special publication of the Taller Gráfica Popular. 1947.
006. Leopoldo Méndez. Detail from a periodical illustration. 1955.
007. Leopoldo Méndez. Illustration for a special publication of the Taller Gráfica Popular. 1951.
008. Leopoldo Méndez or Mariana Yampolsky. Illustration for special publication of the Taller Gráfica Popular. 1949.
009. Jean Charlot. *Death and the X-ray Doctor. Death: "You Remember Me, Doc."* Book illustration. 1951.
010. Jean Charlot. *Death and the Politician. Death: "Don't Strain Yourself, You're In."* Book illustration. 1951.
011. Leopoldo Méndez. Illustration for a special publication of the Taller Gráfica Popular.
012. J. G. Posada Detail from broadside. 1894.
013. M. Manilla. Broadside. Late 19th c.
014. Jean Charlot. *Death and the Pessimist. Death: "You Talked Me Into It."* Book illustration. 1951.
015. Jean Charlot. *Death and the Artist. Death: "Your Prices Will Skyrocket."* Book illustration. 1951.
016. J. G. Posada. *The Calavera of the Trolley Cars.* (The relatively new trolley cars were the cause of many accidents and deaths.) Broadsheet. 1907.
017. M. Manilla. *Calavera of the Eiffel Tower.* Broadsheet. Late 19th c.
018. Alfredo Zalce. *Strangler Calaveras.* Illustration for a special publication of the Taller Gráfica Popular. 1942.
019. Alberto Beltrán. "Circus, Rope, and Theatre." (A comment on the political party PRI). Illustration for a special publication of the Taller Gráfica Popular. 1951.
020. J. G. Posada. Calavera of Don Quixote. Broadside. Early 20th c.
021. Alfredo Zalce. Book illustration. 1946.
022. Alfredo Zalce. Book illustration. 1946.
023. M. Manilla. *Calaveras from Guadalajara.* Broadsheet. Late 19th c.
024. Jean Charlot. *Death . . . Rules the World.* Book illustration. 1951.
025. Atenedoro Pérez y Soto. Book illustration. 1949.
026. Leopoldo Méndez. Illustration for a special publication of the Taller Gráfica Popular.
027. Roberto Montenegro. Book cover. 1936.
028. M. Manilla. *Angel Calavera.* Late 19th c.
029. J. G. Posada. *Dancing the Jarabe in the Other World.* (The jarabe is a popular dance in Mexico.) Broadside. Early 20th c.
030. Roberto Montenegro. Book illustration. 1924.
031. Carlos Neve. Periodical illustration. 1929.
032. Leopoldo Méndez. Illustration for a special publication of the Taller Gráfica Popular.
033. Leopoldo Méndez. Illustration for a special publication of the Taller Gráfica Popular.
034. J. G. Posada. *The Happy Street Cleaner Calaveras.* Broadside. Early 20th c.
035. Ignacio Aguirre. "Without Bread, Land or Money, the Laborer Flees the Country." Periodical illustration. 1952.
036. Carlos Neve. Book illustration. 1947.
037. J. G. Posada. *Happy Calaveras.* Detail from broadside. Early 20th c.
038. M. Manilla. *The Bull Fighting Calavera.* Broadside. Late 19th c.
039. Ignacio Tenorio Suárez. Periodical illustration. 1886.
040. M. Manilla. Periodical illustration. Late 19th c.
041. Ignacio Tenorio Suárez. Periodical illustration. 1886.
042. Roberto Montenegro. Book illustration. 1921.
043. Francisco Diaz de Leon. Book illustration. 1939.
044. Francisco Diaz de Leon. Book illustration. 1939.
045. M. Manilla. *Calaveras at the Running of the Bulls.* Broadsheet. Late 19th c.
046. J. G. Posada. *Calavera Bicyclists.* Broadside. Late 19th c.
047. M. Manilla. Periodical illustration. Late 19th c.
048. Leopoldo Méndez. Illustration for a special publication of the Taller Gráfica Popular.
049. Julio Ruelas. Periodical illustration. 1901.
050. M. Manilla. Periodical illustration. Late 19th c.
051. J. G. Posada. Detail from a broadside representing market women. Early 20th c.
052. J. G. Posada. Detail from a broadside representing market women. Early 20th c.
053. M. Manilla. *The Calavera General of the Graveyard.* Broadside. Late 19th c.
054. Alvin Gill-Tapia. Drawing of a 2005 ceramic sculpture by Carlomagno Pedro Marinez. *The Kiss of Death.*
055. Alvin Gill-Tapia. Drawing of a 1985 wood and papier mâché miniature toy.
056. Alvin Gill-Tapia. Drawing of a 1985 wood and papier mâché miniature toy.
057. Alvin Gill-Tapia. Drawing of a 2005 ceramic sculpture from the studio of the de la Cruz family.
058. Alvin Gill-Tapia. Drawing of a 1990 ceramic candelabra representing Frida Kahlo.
059. Alvin Gill-Tapia. Drawing of a 1990 miniature ceramic figure.
060. M. Manilla. Periodical illustration. Late 19th c.
061. Alvin Gill-Tapia. Drawing of a 1990 miniature ceramic figure.
062. Leopoldo Méndez. Illustration for a special publication of the Taller Gráfica Popular.
063. Figaro. *An Eiffel Tower for the Cemetery of the Illustrated Plans.* Periodical Illustration. 1889.
064. Alvin Gill-Tapia. Drawing of a 2001 papier mâché and wire calavera with flowers and plants growing out of it by Jose Heriberto Sanchez Torres.
065. Alvin Gill-Tapia. Drawing of a 2002 papier mâché and wire groom by Jose Heriberto Sanchez Torres.
066. Alvin Gill-Tapia. Drawing of a 2002 papier mâché and wire bride by Jose Heriberto Sanchez Torres.
067. M. Manilla. *The People's Calavera.* Broadside. Late 19th c.
068. Alvin Gill-Tapia. Drawing of a 2010 ceramic piece by an anonymous artist.
069. M. Manilla. Periodical illustration. Late 19th c.
070. Francisco Moreno Capedevila or Leopoldo Méndez. Book illustration. 1951.
071. J. G. Posada. *Zapatista Calavera.* Broadside. Early 20th c.
072. J. G. Posada. *Alley Cat Calavera.* Broadside. Early 20th c.
073. J. G. Posada. *Calavera of Artists and Artisans.* Early 20th c.
074. Anonymous. Periodical illustration. 1936.
075. J. G. Posada. *Nor Here Will I Forget You.* Detail from broadside, "The Calavera of Cupid." Early 20th c.
076. J. G. Posada. Detail from broadside, "The Big Cemetery of Love." Early 20th c.
077. J. G. Posada. Detail from broadside. Early 20th c.
078. J. G. Posada. Detail from a broadside representing market women. Early 20th c.
079. Anonymous. Detail of periodical illustration. 1936.
080. Anonymous. Calavera of General Huerta, "Tarantula of the North." (Victoriano Huerta fought against the revolutionaries, Villa, Zapata, and others.) Broadside. Early 20th c.
081. J. G. Posada. Detail from broadside, "The Big Cemetery of Love." Early 20th c.
082. J. G. Posada. Detail from broadside, "The Big Cemetery of Love." Early 20th c.
083. Francisco Agüera Bustamante. Book illustration. 1792.
084. Francisco Agüera Bustamante. Book illustration. 1792.
085. Francisco Agüera Bustamante. Book illustration. 1792.
086. Julio Ruelas. Periodical illustration. 1901.
087. J. G. Posada. Detail from broadside, "The Big Cemetery of Love." Early 20th c.
088. J. G. Posada. Detail from broadside, The "Calavera of Cupid." Early 20th c.

089. Leopoldo Méndez. *Arches and Puddles.* Illustration for a special publication of the Taller Gráfica Popular. 1951.

090. Miguel Covarrubias. *Hitler, Mussolini and Hirohito.* Periodical illustration. 1943.

091. Leopoldo Méndez or Mariana Yampolsky. Illustration for special publication of the Taller Gráfica Popular. 1949.

092. Alvin Gill-Tapia. Drawing of a 2001 papier mâché and wire calavera with flowers and plants growing out of it by Jose Heriberto Sanchez Torres.

093. Alvin Gill-Tapia. Drawing of a 1990 miniature altar.

094. J. G. Posada. *The Little Red Devil.* Periodical illustration. 1910.

095. Roberto Montenegro. Book illustration. 1925.

096. Ernesto Guasp. Periodical illustration. 1949.

097. J. G. Posada. Detail from broadside "The Big Cemetery of Love." Early 20th c.

098. J. G. Posada. Detail from broadside. Early 20th c.

099. J. G. Posada. Detail from broadside. Early 20th c.

100. M. Manilla. Periodical illustration. Late 19th c.

101. J. G. Posada. *Twentieth C Calavera.* Early 20th c.

102. J. G. Posada. *Don Ferruco and His Love.* (Don Ferruco was a figure of popular lore in Guadalajara). Detail of broadside, "The Big Cemetery of Love." Early 20th c.

103. J. G. Posada. *Calavera Don Juan Tenorio.* Broadside. 1913.

104. J. G. Posada. Detail from broadside. Early 20th c.

105. J. G. Posada. Detail from broadside. Early 20th c.

106. J. G. Posada. *Pharmacy Calavera.* Early 20th c.

107. Gabriel Fernández Ledesma. Book illustration. 1951.

108. J. G. Posada. *Mole Feast of the Calaveras.* Broadside. 1902.

109. Francisco Mora. Periodical illustration. 1949.

110. Elizabeth Catlett. Periodical illustration. 1949.

111. Francisco Mora. Periodical illustration. 1949.

112. J. G. Posada. Detail from a broadside representing market women. Early 20th c.

113. J. G. Posada. *Melee of the Calavera Paperboys.* Broadside. Early 20th c.

114. J. G. Posada. Card from a lottery game. Early 20th c.

115. Type specimen from the typographic company of Ignacio Cumplido, Mexico City. 1836.

116. J. G. Posada. *The Calavera Catrina.* Broadside. 1913.

117. Type specimen from the typographic company of Ignacio Cumplido, Mexico City. 1836.

118. Gabriel Fernández Ledesma. *J. G. Posada in his Studio.* Magazine cover. 1948.

119. J. G. Posada. *The Dandy.* Broadside. Early 20th c.

120. J. G. Posada. *Calavera Francisco I. Madera.* Broadside. 1910.

121. Anonymous. Book illustration. 1603.

122. M. Manilla. *The Fight for Life.* Broadside. Late 19th c.

123. M. Manilla. *Requiescat in Pace.* Broadside. Late 19th c.

124. Alvin Gill-Tapia. Drawing of a pair of 1999 carved wooden figures.

125. Type specimen from the typographic company of Ignacio Cumplido, Mexico City. 1871.

126. J. G. Posada. Detail from broadside, "The Calavera of Cupid." Early 20th c.

127. J. G. Posada. Detail from broadside, "The Calavera of Cupid." Early 20th c.

128. Gabiel Fernández Ledesma. Magazine Cover. 1948.

129. Alvin Gill-Tapia. Drawing of a 1986 miniature wood and ceramic scene.

130. M. Manilla. Periodical illustration. Late 19th c.

131. Anonymous. Book cover. 1958.

132. Francisco Mora. Periodical illustration. 1949.

133. Type specimen from the typographic company of Ignacio Cumplido, Mexico City. 1836.

134. Gabriel Fernández Ledesma. Book illustration. 1942.

135. M. Manilla. *Calavera Picador.* Broadside. Late 19th c.

136. M. Manilla. *The Calavera of the Happy Widow.* Broadside. Late 19th c.

137. M. Manilla. *Rise From Your Graves Calaveras, The Most Foolhardy of All is Here.* (A reference to the popular play, *Don Juan Tenorio.*) Broadside. Late 19th c.

138. José Clemente Orozco. Periodical illustration. 1925.

139. Gabriel Fernández Ledesma. Drawing of Day of the Dead specialty breads. Magazine illustration. 1948.

140. Gabriel Fernández Ledesma. Drawing of sugar paste figures. Magazine illustration. 1948.

141. Anonymous. Book illustration. 1953.

142. José Clemente Orozco. Book illustration. 1931.

143. Anonymous. Periodical illustration. 1955.

144. Miguel Covarrubias. Book illustration. 1947.

145. Anonymous. Periodical illustration. 1936.

146. Anonymous. Periodical illustration. 1955.

147. Anonymous. Flyer. 1965.

148. Alberto Beltrán. Book cover. 1954.

149. J. G. Posada. *Calavera Adelita.* (The women soldiers of the revolution were known as Adelitas.) Broadside. Early 20th c.

150. J. G. Posada. Detail from broadside. Early 20th c.

151. Anonymous. Periodical illustration. 1936.

152. Lola Cueto. Book illustration. 1947.

153. Angel Zamarripa. *Portrait of J. G. Posada with Catrina and Devil.* Periodical cover. 1952.

154. J. G. Posada. Cover of chapbook. Early 20th c.

155. Miguel Covarrubias. *The Bread of the Dead.* Book illustration. 1947

156. Alberto Beltrán. Book illustration. 1963.

157. M. Manilla. Card for a lottery game. Late 19th c.

158. M. Manilla. Periodical illustration. Late 19th c.

159. M. Manilla. Periodical illustration. Late 19th c.

160. Leopoldo Méndez. Illustration for a special publication of the Taller Gráfica Popular.

161. J. G. Posada. *Calavera of the War of the French Intervention.* Broadsheet. Early 20th c.

162. Francisco Morena Capedevila. Book illustration. 1951.

163. Alejandro Rosales. Book illustration. 1967.

164. Julio Prieto. Book illustration. 1945.

165. Roberto Montenegro. The Death of Don Quixote. Book illustration. 1921.

166. Andrea Gómez. Periodical illustration. 1957.

167. Jean Charlot. Book illustration. 1951.

168. Leopoldo Méndez. Book illustration. 1951.

169. Alberto Beltrán. Book illustration. 1952.

170. Francisco Moreno Capdevila. Book illustration. 1954.

171. Leopoldo Méndez. Lithograph. 1950.

172. J. G. Posada. Detail from broadside. Early 20th c.

173. Alvin Gill-Tapia. Drawing of a 1989 ceramic Calavera dog.

174. Alvin Gill-Tapia. Drawing of a 1989 ceramic Calavera dog.

175. Francisco Moreno Capedevila or Leopoldo Méndez. Book illustration. 1951.

176. Julio Prieto. Book Illustration. 1947.

177. Gabriel Fernández Ledesma. Periodical illustration. 1962.

178. Mariano Martinez. Book illustration. 1933.

179. Alberto Beltrán or Adolfo Mexiac. Periodical illustration. 1955.

180. J. G. Posada. *Flirtation Between the Chickpea Seller and the Water Carrier.* Broadside. Early 20th c.

181. Gabriel Fernández Ledesma. Book illustration. 1941.

182. Alberto Beltrán or Leopoldo Méndez. Detail from illustration. Special publication of the Taller Gráfica Popular. 1956.

183. Leopoldo Méndez. Illustration for a special publication of the Taller Gráfica Popular.

184. Anonymous. Periodical illustration. 1878.

185. J. G. Posada. Detail from broadside, "The Calavera of Cupid." Early 20th c.

186. Anonymous. *The Calavera Zapata.* Broadside. Early 20th c.

187. J. G. Posada. *Revolutionary Calavera from Oaxaca.* Broadside. Early 20th c.